A LOOK BACK AT

OLD KIRKCALDY

Carol McNeill

First published 2014

ISBN 978-0-9534686-9-0

Published by
Fife Publicity
fifepublicity@btinternet.com
www.carolmcneill.co.uk

Printed by
Multiprint (Scotland) Limited, Kirkcaldy
Telephone 01592 204755
www.multiprint.tv

Acknowledgements:

The majority of the images in this book are from the Jim Swan postcard collection.
Many thanks to Kirkcaldy Civic Society for the generous use of a selection of their
postcards; Kirkcaldy Galleries for the images of the Philp Schools; and Photopolis.org
for images on page 4 (top) and page 18 (top). The remainder of the illustrations are
from the author's own postcard collection.

Introduction

Kirkcaldy in the early years of the 20th century was a very different place than it is now. Smaller of course, with old buildings which though picturesque had very little in the way of modern sanitation, and private shops which sold everything that modern supermarkets do now. A business directory listed around 150 trades and professions in the town: as well as the familiar linen manufacturers, engineers and ironfounders, physicians, newsagents and restaurants, there were more esoteric businesses such as a girth web manufacturer, a servants' registry, umbrella makers and a taxidermist.

Postcards produced at the time give us an accurate picture of what the town looked like in the early 1900s. And if trams seem to play a central role in many of the postcards, this was no accident: the town was tremendously proud of its tramway system, the first in Fife and indeed one of the first in the UK. It ran from 1903 until May 1931, when depreciating rolling stock and the advent of buses put an end to the service. A contemporary guide book said:

"Nothing that our Corporation has taken in hand, and pushed through in the public interest, has been done so effectively or proved a source of such pleasurable surprise to every member of our community as our tram cars. Very few accidents have occurred since the cars commenced running, and considering the narrowness of the streets and the congested traffic at times, this state of affairs reflects credit upon the motormen. During the year ending 1905, the number of passengers carried totalled over three million, or in other words, the population of Kirkcaldy was carried 107 times during the year."

However, not everything that was happening in the town was subject to such praise, with the condition of the foreshore causing particular concern. "Nothing could better exemplify the rest-and-be-thankful policy of the Town Council than the ruinous condition of the road and sands. The constant war going on between the sea and the rubbish heaps keeps the otherwise beautiful sands in a vile state." The building of the promenade and sea wall in 1923 however put an end to that complaint.

Building the Post Office on the corner of Hunter Street and Wemyssfield was also unpopular. Before the present Town House was built, a large mansion house and grounds belonging to Sir Thomas Elder was across the road. "In building the new Post Office on the site it occupies in a side street, the inhabitants of Kirkcaldy are conscious that the Post Office authorities consulted their own convenience in preference to that of the public. It is a subject of much public regret that such a handsome building has been thrust into a corner where its well-balanced proportions can be viewed from no point of vantage."

A great deal of that old Kirkcaldy has gone: but much of it still remains for those who take the trouble to look.

Seafield Tower was built probably in the middle of the 16th century as a square tower house by the Moultray family. Now registered as a B-listed category building, it fell into disrepair many years ago.

Kirkcaldy's beach beside the Tiel Burn was a favourite place for picnics. Although most of the factory chimneys were in the distance, there were two factories nearby making lemonade, herb beer and shandy as well as Brown's shipyard.

Sands Road on the shore had become a general rubbish dump. It was replaced by the promenade and sea wall, first suggested in 1904 but not completed until 1923 as a project to give work to unemployed men.

The new prom construction and beach were enthusiastically welcomed, and soon proved a popular spot for locals and visitors especially on sunny Sunday afternoons.

The junction of Nicol Street and High Street is still recognisable today, with the curved premises of what was then the Links Bread Society and the imposing Wemyss Buildings still remaining.

The west end of the High Street is pictured before the advent of the tramcars. Kirkcaldy and District Equitable Co-op is on the right, with the steeples of Abbotsrood Church on the same side and the Congregational church opposite.

Shops in the 1900s included Michie's grocer's which sold Mazawattee tea and Balwearie brand of whisky; Buchan's Beehive which made hats and umbrellas; and Peebles the chemist which sold everything from elastic stockings to castor oil.

Duncan's stationers at 19 High Street, with an advert at roof level, included a printing and bookbinding service. Its adjoining West End studio took carefully posed studio photographs of weddings and family groups.

Beveridge Park was formed from ninety acres of land purchased by Kirkcaldy Town Council from the Raith estate as part of the £50,000 bequest from Provost Michael Beveridge.

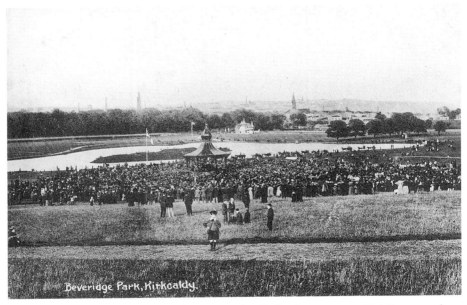

More than 10,000 people flocked to Beveridge Park when it was officially opened on 24 September 1892 by Mrs Beveridge, widow of the donor, along with the Provost, magistrates and Town Council.

The bandstand was the focal point for the park's opening ceremony. It was also a popular venue for local bands which played on Sunday afternoons to appreciative audiences.

Feeding the Swans, Beveridge Park – Kirkcaldy

The park swans which were always well fed by visitors co-existed happily with the small boats in the park lake in this image from the Twenties or Thirties.

THE LOCH, BEVERIDGE PARK, KIRKCALDY.

Beveridge Park lake has always been a popular spot with small boats for hire. An early version of the ice cream van can be seen in the foreground with a white-coated salesman and his cart.

Kirkcaldy.
Abbotshall Road.

4076. 6.

Abbotshall Road is still recognisable today, although the tram lines have disappeared. The original Abbotshall Church was built on this site in 1674 and the grave of child prodigy Marjory Fleming is in the churchyard.

THE OLD BARNEY JAIL,
BELL WYND, KIRKCALDY.

The house and adjoining jail at 124 Links Street, at the corner of Bell Wynd, were the premises of the Baron Baillie, law officer and judge. At that time Linktown was a separate burgh from Kirkcaldy with its own justice system. Prisoners' cells were situated behind the curved outside stair, and the bell on the roof was rung on special occasions including the Armistice at the end of WWI.

Another view of Links Street with the Baron Baillie's house on the right. When Linktown became part of Kirkcaldy, there was no longer a need for a separate legal system and the building ended its days as a book shop before being demolished.

Market Place in Links Street was the traditional site for the stalls and side shows of the annual Links Market before they moved on to the Prom along with the larger rides. The entrance gates of the Methven Pottery complex can be seen beside the tramcar.

This view over the Links includes remains of a harbour and railway planned for Seafield in 1891. Although 16 acres of quay space were intended to ship 8000 tons of local coal a day, only one pier was built before the project was abandoned.

Baillie Robert Philp who died in 1828 left a Trust Fund to build four schools - three in Kirkcaldy and one in Kinghorn. The children received free education, school books and clothes. The Linktown School was surmounted by a statue of Baillie Philp with the figure of a child on each side.

Pinder's two circuses were regular attractions at the Links Market and included lions, clowns, acrobats and an elephant at their traditional stance in the basin at the west end of the esplanade.

Bridge Street now has a very different appearance from this old image. Hendry's spinning mill on the left was just one of the buildings which were demolished in the 1950s, along with the adjacent Brown's Close and Horse Wynd.

The Belgian owner of Descampes Garage sold high quality cars including Mercedes and Darracq. They advertised their services as 'driving tuition, battery charging, and repairs with skilled workmen sent to any part of the country'. The building later became the Station Hotel.

The Adam Smith Halls and Beveridge Library with its free reading room were also built from the legacy of Provost Michael Beveridge. The building was opened in October 1899 by philanthropist Andrew Carnegie, who also donated a fine pipe organ.

The railway came to Kirkcaldy in 1847, and the first station buildings included overhead canopies above the platforms. Some of the town's many factories were built beside the railway to take advantage of convenient and quick transport of goods.

Kirkcaldy Station.

This image of Kirkcaldy railway station dates to around 1910 and shows a steam train arriving at the platform. The chimney of Barry, Ostlere and Shepherd's linoleum works can be seen on the left.

Balsusney House adjacent to the railway station was donated to the town by owner John Maxton to be used as a site for the town's War Memorial, and was demolished to make way for the new building.

WAR MEMORIAL AND GROUNDS, KIRKCALDY.
OPENED JUNE 27TH 1925.

The museum and art gallery were gifted in 1925 as part of the War Memorial by linoleum manufacturer John Nairn, whose son was killed in WWI. Factory buildings including the linoleum works of Barry, Ostlere and Shepherd can be seen in the background.

This early image of the High Street was taken on a hot day, with several shops putting out awnings to shade their goods from the sun. Ferguson's bootmaker's was on the left with a barber's opposite with a sign advertising hair cutting, shampooing and shaving saloons.

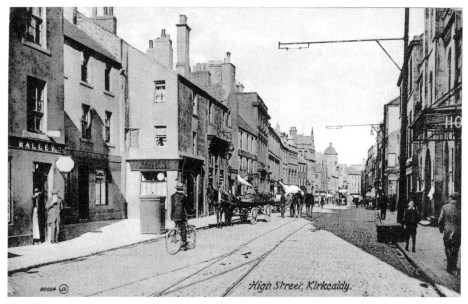

Several different forms of transport were used in the High Street, with a bicycle, horses and carts, and a tram all using the road. Shops on the left included McCathie's grocer's shop and Constable's the watch makers, with the George Hotel on the right.

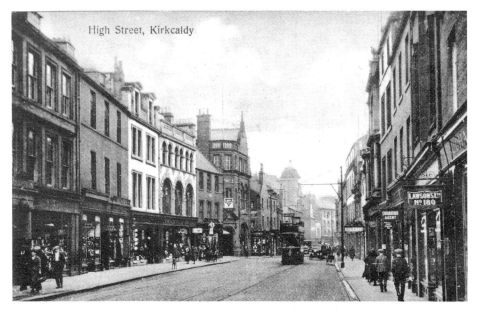

High Street, Kirkcaldy

The distinctive YMCA, built as a memorial to Provost Patrick Don Swan, is on the corner of Kirk Wynd with a painter on trestles freshening up a shop sign on the other corner. The Rialto cinema was across the road along with an emigration agent.

Passsers-by, including young delivery boys, obligingly posed for the photographer. The tram carried an advert for Barnet and Morton's large store in the High Street which then sold a comprehensive range of household goods including mangles, clocks, ornaments and linoleum.

Kirk Wynd is still recognisable today, with the Old Kirk at the top of the hill. The shop on the right is Payne's Boot Depot with a notice saying 'Terms cash. Repairs neatly done'. One of the youngsters is delivering a basket with bottles of beer.

The Famous Kirk Wynd – Kirkcaldy

Thomas Carlyle, writer and scholar, lived in the house with the outside stair in Kirk Wynd when he was appointed headmaster of the Burgh School across the road in Hill Street in 1816.

The crowds of men on foot and on bicycles were streaming out from McIntosh's furniture factory in Victoria Road which opened in the 1890s and operated on the site until the firm moved to new premises in 1970.

A horse and carriage trotting beside a tram provided a contrasting view of old and new forms of transport in Victoria Road. Kirkcaldy's tramway system was installed in 1903 and was hugely popular until buses took over in 1931.

This view of St Brycedale Avenue has not altered much, with the Adam Smith Halls on the left, the Police Station across the road, and the spire of St Brycedale Church in the background.

Kirkcaldy's Police Station was built in 1901 at a cost of £27,000. It was described at the time as incorporating cells, a jailor's house, and 'a court room with a ceiling enriched with tracery work of leaves, and scales symbolising Justice on the walls'.

The Burgh School, built in 1843 to replace an earlier school in Hill Street, was originally a single storey building with Greek-style pillars in front. When the building was extended 50 years later by Michael Barker Nairn, the façade of the ground floor was incorporated into the building.

St Brycedale United Free Church was built in 1881 after the previous church in Tolbooth Street became too small for its congregation. The Burgh School after it had been remodelled can be seen on the right in this view from West Albert Road.

The County Buildings, as the Sheriff Court was originally called, were built in Whytescauseway in 1894 at a cost of £9,000. An early guidebook said: 'Courts in connection with the county as distinct from the burgh are held here, and the Sheriff Clerk has his offices on the premises.'

As the trams had a route up Whytescauseway as well as running in both directions along the High Street, there was often congestion at the junction while the drivers negotiated past each other.

Sailors' Walk, built in the 15th and 16th centuries, was originally a group of several houses. It was saved from possible demolition in the 1930s when a far-seeing local committee launched a public appeal to save it. The building was taken over in 1935 by the National Trust for Scotland, which gradually restored it to its former glory until its completion after WWII. Several royal visitors over the years may have stayed there, and it's thought that Mary of Guise and her daughter Mary, Queen of Scots, may have stopped there. Many original features were uncovered almost intact, including wooden beams inscribed with Biblical texts, fleur-de-lis and thistles on the walls in plaster, a bed which slid into a stone recess, and a ceiling decorated with fish and flowers.

Shops at the Port Brae in the 1930s included Gillies the furniture store and the Army Club on the right. St James' Church in the background was built in 1862 but fell into disrepair and was demolished in 1970.

Thomas Reilly's salt works were situated at 360 High Street at the foot of Coal Wynd. The salt would originally have been made by a process of evaporation from salt pans on the shore near St James' Church, and later by refining rock salt.

Promenade Sea Wall, Kirkcaldy, from the Harbour.

The new prom construction ended at Port Brae where it was landscaped with a series of curved steps which provided a pleasant place to sit in the sun. The Port Brae cinema behind was one of the town's many cinemas at that time.

The Bucket Pats, Kirkcaldy.

The Bucket Pats, at the east end of the prom near St James' Church, was a natural rocky basin which filled at high tide with sea water utilised by the salt works. It became a popular area with local children for paddling and sand castles.

Kirkcaldy had a harbour as early as the 16th century, and James V sailed from it to France to bring back his bride Madeleine of Valois. This tall-masted ship was one of many which tied up at the harbour, with Sailors' Walk across the road from the quayside.

This section of the harbour was locally known as the 'wee pier' as small boats from the local sailing club and smaller ships were able to tie up easily there. St James' Church can be seen in the background.

At the Harbour, Kirkcaldy

A branch railway line was built on the harbour in 1849 to increase opportunities for commercial traffic, particularly for the linoleum industry. The small building on the left housed the mechanism to raise the railway bridge to let ships through.

AT THE HARBOUR, KIRKCALDY.

As the town's industries decreased and factories closed down, trade diminished and the harbour lay unused for many years in the late 20th century. It has recently re-opened to commercial shipping servicing the expanding flour mill at the foot of the Path.

The Docks, Kirkcaldy   T. G. Blyth, Kirkcaldy

Records from 1834 show that the *Enterprise* and the *Fifeshire* sailed regularly from Kirkcaldy harbour to London, the *Eliza Burns* and the *Isabella Black* were on the Newcastle run, and there were daily sailings to Edinburgh and Glasgow. A new pier and wet dock were begun in 1843, and a large harbour extension was begun in 1906 when Provost Barnet laid a commemoration stone. The first plan costing £300,000 was considered too expensive, and the work was completed in 1909 at a cost of £140,000, with the Earl of Elgin performing the opening ceremony. The official opening was by the *SS Kirkcaldy* owned by linen manufacturer Major HL Stocks, but the first ship to inadvertently make history by entering the new extension was a sailing ship loaded with timber.

The Prom and esplanade extended from west to east for the whole length of the waterfront, covering up the site of the old Bucket Pats.

The Union Church at the foot of the Path was formed after a disruption in the church and was built in 1824. Although it closed its doors in 1928, the façade still remains and is part of the buildings of Fife College.

Although the Path had been given a series of improvements in the late 1800s, it was still a very steep and narrow road in the 1900s. It was a difficult uphill journey for trams as well as a hazard for horse-drawn traffic, and several vehicles came to grief on the hill.

KIRKCALDY.

This overview from the top of the Path takes in Kirkcaldy harbour and some of the many factories which were operational at the time, including the curved frontage of Nairn's factory opposite the harbour.

The Cottage Hospital was gifted by Michael Barker Nairn and opened officially by the Earl of Rosslyn in 1890, with a circular extension added later. An estate of private houses now stands on the site.

Pathhead United Free Church at the foot of St Clair Street was the subject of a bitter dispute in 1905 when the building was handed over to the 'Wee Free' Church in Pathhead, leaving the UF congregation to hold their services in a nearby public hall. High flats were later built on the same spot.

Nether Street, Kirkcaldy.

Nether Street in Pathhead has changed beyond all recognition, with the demolition of the factories and most of the old and picturesque houses on nearby Weavers Row and Ross Terrace.

Another of Robert Philp's schools was in Nether Street under the supervision of headmaster Mr Arthur. After the school was closed in 1892, Nairn's expanded their factory and built right round it. When the linoleum works were demolished in 1967, the school buildings and commemorative plaque were found to be intact.

Mid Street, parallel to Commercial Street (then known as Back Street) was once a busy neighbourhood with a mixture of houses and shops, including a licensed grocer, fish restaurant and William Walker's boot and warehouse.

Mid Street, Kirkcaldy.

The distinctive outside stairs and gas lamps in some of the houses in Mid Street in the early 1900s have long gone, as have the shops including a butcher and draper. Mid Street was once the venue for the annual Pathhead Market.

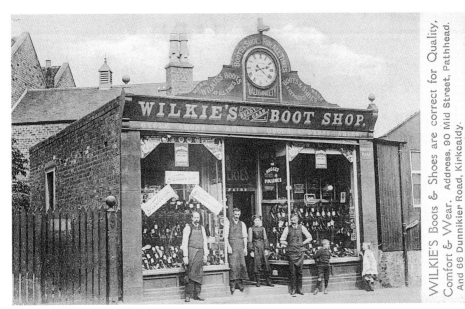

Wilkie's Boot Shop had a branch at 90 Mid Street as well as in this building at 66 Dunnikier Road. They advertised that their boots and shoes, which included cycle shoes and dress shoes, were correct for quality, comfort and wear.

Commercial Street, with the tower of Pathhead Hall and Wilson's Refreshment Rooms. The curved building on the corner was the very first shop set up in 1904 by the Buttercup Dairy Company which built up 250 branches throughout the UK over 25 years.

Loughborough Road Church was opened in 1881 as a United Presbyterian church, and later became Church of Scotland. The main building was demolished in 1985 with the hall remaining as a place of worship.

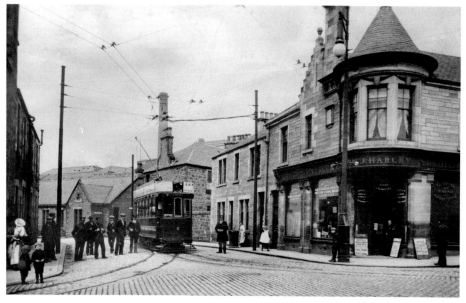

The corner of Junction Road and St Clair Street is still recognisable today although the cobbles and tramlines are long gone. Mrs Harley's shop on the corner was a newsagent, bookseller, fancy goods shop and a tobacconist selling Tam O'Shanter tobacco and Prize Crop cigarettes.

Overton Road, with a motor delivery van from Kirkcaldy Bakeries in Links Street stopped at the corner grocery shop. Two boys in a small pony and trap had little traffic to hold them up.

The Gallatown tram terminus was the boundary for Kirkcaldy trams, and thereafter single-decker yellow trams - nicknamed the mustard boxes - run by Wemyss and District Tramways continued the route to Leven.

Dunnikier house was owned by the Oswald family whose mansion house was at the top of the Path. They moved to a town house in Oswald's Wynd until James Oswald, MP for Kirkcaldy Burgh, built Dunnikier House in the late 18th century.

Entrance to Dunnikier Den, Kirkcaldy

Dunnikier Den was the entrance to Dunnikier estate, and the ornate gates beside the lodge house - originally called Octavia Lodge - were popularly known as the Golden Gates.

Raith House, Kirkcaldy.

Raith House was built in the 17th century for Alexander Melville, and became the property of Ronald Crawford Munro-Ferguson, MP for Leith Burghs. The grounds were often used for Sunday School trips and works' outings.

JAMES ADAMS, Publisher]   RAITH BAND CONTEST 1905.   [Balfour Street, Kirkcaldy.

The Raith Estate also hosted the annual brass band contest which drew huge numbers of spectators to hear bands from all over Scotland and the north of England. Kirkcaldy Horticultural Society, which organised the competition, held their annual flower show on the same day.

Ravenscraig Castle with its two round towers was commissioned in 1460 by King James II of Scotland at an estimated cost then of £665. Although the king died before it was completed, his widow Mary of Gueldres probably occupied it for a few years. Its high rocky position overlooking the Forth made it ideal for defence, and it was one of the first castles in Scotland specifically built for defence from gunfire from the sea with some walls fourteen feet thick.

RAVENSCRAIG PARK, KIRKCALDY.
GIFTED BY SIR MICHAEL NAIRN, BART. OPENED ON 29TH JUNE 1929.

Ravenscraig Park was gifted to the town by Sir Michael Nairn after he bought Dysart House and policies from the 5th Earl of Rosslyn who lost the estate after his spectacular lifestyle of gambling and racehorses left him bankrupt.

RAVENSCRAIG CASTLE, KIRKCALDY.

Ravenscraig Castle saw many royal visitors in its early days, including James IV of Scotland and his son James V with his second wife Mary of Guise, the mother of Mary, Queen of Scots.

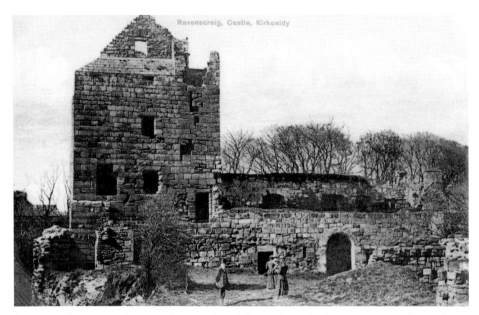

A group of amateur photographers explored the castle with their cameras and tripods. In the early 1900s the castle grounds were open to the public on New Year's Day to play pitch and toss and a traditional game 'a bawbee she kyles'.

Gardeners in Ravenscraig Park planted out this carefully designed floral clock. The clock hands were set to show the time that the park closed each evening.

Chapel village was once a rural hamlet quite separate from Kirkcaldy until it was amalgamated within the town boundary. The land originally belonged to the Oswalds of Dunnikier, and the houses would have been for estate workers.

Many of the buildings, including a smiddy, in the foreground of this image of Chapel village have since been demolished. The houses in the centre of the village mostly remained intact and are still mainly recognisable today.